COURSING

by
Kenneth Weene

Dedicated to

my wonderful wife and muse, Rosalyn,
and with thanks to those special poets and friends who have
helped me to hone my craft, especially my editor C. Christy
White.

COURSING
Table of Contents

RELIQUARY

Boxes in the attic

filled with photographs,
people I had never seen:
my parents, happy, in bathing costumes
on boardwalk Revere beach;
father smiling and his parents,
whom I never knew,
despite monthly visits
to be kissed with grandmother's old-age musk.

No pictures of Benjamin,
father's brother
who died young
and was never mentioned.
Memory of the dead is a luxury
we were taught to scorn.

Had he lived, perhaps the family rage
would have burned less hot.
If there had been time for tears,
perhaps father's cries would have
extinguished the flames.

Hiding from mother's protection,
I played solitaire with fading photographs.
Who went with whom?
Where did they go?
I never asked.

When they were dead,
the last casket mourned,
I asked cousins who recalled
a different grandmother,
one who gave love with food,
strudel and gefilte fish,
and sang bobeli Yiddish songs.

In the boxes of photographs
uncles and aunts
graduations and cousins
but no Benjamin.
There were no photographs of tears.

Only smiles
worn like new clothes
and stiff Sabbath shoes,
an un-kissed mezuzah.

He wrote to defy the guards and challenge
the gods

the prisoner in his flimsy striped suit
and flip-flop shoes used a mix of urine
and frass on bits of paper salvaged from the wind
blown from the city to the east
where he had lived, where his ghost
might someday haunt. He wrote with a stick
sharpened and dipped in the greenish liquid,
non-ink. Blowing to dry the simple,
squiggled words of his day spent yearning
for a glimpse, for a listening ear,
for a quick embrace.
Words stuffed into the lice and bed-bug
mattress straw to be burned on the day of release,
when the priest, dressed in white,
would absolve his sins.

Posthumous pardon offers no reprieve
to his children who'll receive
a formal certificate which again
brings tears. Such letters resurrect
the dead so mourners can remember and weep.
No parole, just permission to recall the undead,
permission to let him go.

> My Gap-dressed grandson splashed
> in the wavelets and chased snipe
> with *wahoo* and *watch me*.
> He laughed as the birds hopped about;
> then into the air, a half-eaten snail dripping

from one mouth, a frenzy of guano from
another orifice. The whir; wings beating
frantic escape. *Hop-it, Hop-it* they called
in fright. What made him, only five, a
torturer? Is it humanity at our worst?

In school they bullied him for his lazy eye
and called him names to blindside him
on the jungle gym. He no longer wanted
to go to the park. Brooding, he'd throw
his Thomas tank engine across the room.
I don't care became his favorite words.
About himself or others, who can say?

The burial pits were filled with those too weary,
those who could not climb back to the surface.
Drowning on land with sand and soil the last
breath untaken the last sound un-sighed.
He is there and the bits of paper turned
to ash and black smoke. We do not have
a pope, only the dead. Sprinkled lime
and the odor remains.
Half a day's work, the satisfied guards
march back to their barracks,
then to lunch. They drink a beer
and laugh at him;
his last desperate struggle
met with a shovel. *Did he bleed?*
 Like a pig. They eat ham and cabbage.
The prisoners who live
receive cabbage soup. Perhaps today
they will find a leaf.

Holocaust Rag

When the world collapses in on us with a painful final
    thud,
I'll look at you in wonderment and ask if it is love.
Will you love me then, my dear;
and will I still love you
when the chatter and cacophony
of life have all been stilled?
The mountainside of history has tipped upon its side
to crush the sobbing breath from these our empty lives -
leaving us but the chance to die in a merry burst of sighs.

The tap, jack, hammer of their marching boots
the sounds of windows breaking -
glass beneath their feet.
I'll turn to you in wonder then
and ask with new resolve
if you'll always love me
though we shall not grow old.

The bullets whining by us sound like honey bees
searching for sweet flowers to court on bended wings.
How strange the martial music sounds
at the very end of things:
the tuba umphing melancholy,
the crying hurt of strings!
When the world collapses in on us with a painful final
    thud,
I'll look at you in wonderment and ask if it is love.
Will you love me then, my dear;
and will I still love you;

will our love have meaning
when our world is through?

In the piled high of bodies
being mined for toothless gold
we'll search for each other
in the terror of our souls.
Twisted in agony the final torture comes
with the whispered hiss of gas from the shower heads
    above.
In quick lime trenches
unmarked the bodies lie -
tortured by a hatred which has refused to die.
When the tap, jack, hammer
of the leather wearied boots
has faded from memory except in history books,
the soulless echo of their tread
in the silent streets remains.
When the world collapses in on us with a painful final
    thud,
I'll look at you in wonderment and ask if it is love.
Will you love me then, my dear;
and will I still love you?

In the quiet of an afternoon,
we walked and talked and laughed.
We kissed beneath a lilac bush
in the pleasant, little park.
I held your hand in mine in a slow and carefree way.
We did not want to listen;
we did not want to know.
It was enough to smell the lilac tree's bouquet.

The scent of rotting bodies worming in the sun,
the scent of rotting bodies, that had not begun.
Pawing through the pile,
wrapped in wretched rags,
searching for my lover -
in my heart I asked:
When the world collapses in on us with a painful final
    thud,
I'll look at you in wonderment and ask if it is love.
Will you love me then, my dear;
and will I still love you?

The wide sunk eyes of children -
starving shrunken frames -
hold a fascination for those who never saw
the walking dead in torment shuffling along.
Each painful step a question crying out to god.
There were no thundered answers,
no plagues, no fiery guides -
only the unwept salt of tears
from those too tired to cry.

In the decadence of my poetry,
in the anger of my art,
I ask and get no answers
to my repeated "whys?"
If we had passed our lives walking hand in hand
passing through the lilac park and listening to the band
playing umpah-umpah-pah on their white and tidy stand,
then I would not have to ask each atonement day
will you love me then, my dear;
and will I still love you

when the song is finished,
when the day is through?

Pirate burial

I carry memories like canvas wrapped pirates
to the tidal marsh, where the sea has ebbed
and left scurrying crabs, sea cucumbers, and wood
worn gray as worrying thoughts,
to be buried before the next high tide.

   In Poznan, Poland, gravestones
   from the Jewish cemetery
   were used by Nazis to reinforce
   the walls of the city's lake—
   no Juden to remain;
   all memory removed.

During that war, a sailor and his wife
lived in our spare bedroom and half bath.
He played with me, a toddler,
tumbling on the floor, stealing my love,
holding me in great swooping arms.
I cried when the sailor was deployed,
no longer available for pony rides
or somersaults. No longer there for me.

Years later I met the sailor again.
A quick visit at their home
on Long Island. Still married,
children, happy together.
A patch covered one eye
lost somewhere in the Pacific.
His arms shrunk from memories.

Old and young, men and women,
the Jewish slaves perished in the cold lake
burying those gravestones,
burying those memories,
burying all traces of families,
of generations.
They in turn were buried in ditches.
Never hypocrites just bureaucrats,
the Nazis erected no monuments, no
                    stones
just recorded numbers instead of names.

I wish that sailor had carried me,
like the great stork of Polish folktales,
on his back to a new country.
I cried again that evening knowing he had not.
How has that memory resurfaced? Better
to add ballast to those hemp-tied sails.
Pirate ghosts can steal something more valuable
than gold doubloons and pieces of eight.

Waiting for the Messiah

Steam completes the room
       condenses on the yellow-tinged walls
       slithers to the tile floor.
Wet with sweat and condensation—
       big bellies pouting out—
we talk about sports and politics
about weather and our gods.
The snake-hissed steam memories—
generations now remote—
       lost,
           diasporic ghosts.
Grandfathers ladle water on their heads
unmindful—
       or afraid—
of the shower on the wall.
It is holy water they ladle—
       blessed by all those wasted lives.
In Belarus
       grandfathers' blood
           washed dirt streets
               while the synagogues
                   in flames and ash
proclaimed,
       Messiah, do not dare to pass.

Somerville, Massachusetts, 1946

> "there on the beaches of
> Normandy I began to reflect on
> the wonders of these ordinary
> people whose lives were laced
> with the markings of greatness."
> — Tom Brokaw, <u>The Greatest
> Generation</u>

Italian bakeries have no business making French eclairs
and zeppole should not morph into doughnuts
filled with strawberry jam so sweet
that only coffee drinkers can survive.
Still, my uncle the pediatrician,
who endured the war and earned a bronze star,
could not resist buying three of each;
noshing as he rode through Somerville
making babies well and urging mothers
to feed their children healthy food:
bacon and eggs, whole milk,
buttered toast, and orange juice.

He climbed stairs with a black bag and little else
except the recent miracle of penicillin.
No mold grew on those bakery treats.
No time for that. Consumed
before his rounds were done.
At each home, he'd stop for coffee,
fresh perked, two sugars, and cream.
You make fresh for the doctor who comes
even when he knows you cannot pay.
You make a special effort and bake

a little something, cookies for his children,
cannoli, perhaps a cake.

He does not bring them home. *Not
healthy* he reminds himself when he stops
and gives them to his friend, the optometrist,
who stayed stateside and has no children.
The next day, patients having their eyes checked,
get treats. But, never eclairs or doughnuts
filled to oozing overflow
with sweet, blood-red, strawberry jam.

Elm

I was only five that first day.
We arrived late afternoon
at the old farmhouse in Maine.
Looking up, I beheld gentle titans
bestriding the hilltop.
While other trees and even people
towered over me, these giant
elms—my father called them—
scraped the clouds,
and hid the sun with shade.

Climb them?
I could not have reached the first branch
even perched on my father's shoulders.
I imagined the eagle's nest I was sure to find
were I, by magic, lifted to that canopy
of distant leaves which rustled
in a breeze redolent of adventure, excitement,
and childish fear of so much unknown.

Had those tender giants not been on guard,
I would not have wandered off.
Down the hill I trotted,
sure that I could find my way.
Only look up and see them wave,
follow their graceful arms.

Don Quimby, a massive, chain-smoking man,
who logged the mountain and hauled felled trees
across the frozen pond

even after his dozer had fallen through the ice,
wanted to cut those elms.
One tree could yield a house
and the wood to keep its Franklin stove
warm all winter long.
Dad, thinking of parents on visitors' day, declined.
It wasn't love of nature, which never stopped him
from shooting whippoorwills, skunk—odiferous
    mistake—
or a porcupine searching for bark beetles
high in a crook of great, curved titan limbs.

I had at ten lost those dearest friends.
Disease ravished the elm; their wood
could no longer be used, especially not burned.
Sawmills laid off men, and Don,
for all the white pine still to cut,
took on more dozer work.
Locals riled against the Dutch as if they had blame
and cursed the modernity of international trade.

In a bleak funeral procession,
I walked around each pillar now devoid of sap,
beneath each crown gone from green
to yellow and then to naught but brittle twigs.

My father paid Don to cut the dead,
to cart away those quiet timber folks,
to leave stumps too close to earth to make a bench.
A plinth for childhood's memories
suitable for fairies and little folk to stage their dance.

Pukwudgie

That first night in Maine, I knew there were little people
          about:
elves, gnomes, fairies, leprechauns, perhaps a pukwudgie
driven from the Bay Colony by determined Puritans.
There had to be, for their lanterns danced about the lawn.
My brother wanted to imprison them in jars, but I
          followed
down the paths, straining to hear their movements
in the leaves and duff. Next morning searching the dew-
grass for footprints to prove they had visited in the night.

Sometimes, in June, before the campers and counselors
came and there was naught to scare our visitors away,
I could hear them dancing about the elms and holding
          court
beneath the white birch. Who else would dare
to tear away the bark? No doubt proclamations, ukase
from Oberon, Titania's brayed letters of love.

Each time I was sure they were at hand, the little folk
disappeared. Chipmunks darted; cheeks puffed with nuts.
Occasionally a robin or a swallow chittered with
          concern.
But, those magical dwellers of the forest had cloaked
themselves invisible. I listened to their mocking laughs.
everywhere just down the path, behind that tree.

Following the brook that boundaried our land, I found
their lair. Tadpoles, polliwogs, fleck-skinned pickerel,
dragon- and damselflies, flitting just out of reach,

tempting the fish to leap with glittering stomach
and subtle splash. I sat for hours on a moss-covered rock.
Hues changed crepuscule and darkness came.
When I could no longer see, I'm sure I heard them leave,
to make love among the ferns,
                              to dance about the trees.

Silence

I carried my toy cannon everywhere.
Fired it shouting *bang* and *boom*.
Built a fort from cushions and waited
to defend my grandfather
against the advancing German army.

    Adults whispered about the Shoah.
    the great wind sweeping Europe
    leaving us Jews without a Golam.

    Only one demon allowed at a time
    in this world

    goose-stepping our relatives into camps.

    What kind of wind kills Jews?
    Why doesn't god intervene?
    Either god has no ears
       or…
           just doesn't listen to Jewish prayers.

My mother, fearful of the world,
       locked me on the porch;
the railing too high to be seen,
       too high for me to see.

I sat in a corner and crayoned rage
until the wasp attack raised my screams.

    Did the *kinder* of Europe scream?

Did they have toy guns and pillow fortresses?

Had they lived, would they
have been overprotected by mothers
who took their toy guns as my mother
had taken mine?

Too much violence.

When my uncle brought us
to the Watertown Arsenal
to see great guns being made,
I remembered my toy.

My cousin wailed in fright.
Was it those monstrous weapons,
or the bangs and booms of machines,
or the knowledge that it could happen
that terrified him?

In school we learned cursive,
were told to hide under desks
when we heard the bomb,
saw the blinding light.

Our family never talked about the wind,
the camps. Never mentioned God.

The buried can no longer be ignored.

A toy cannon screams against the wind.

Memorial for my grandfather, Ike, and the wartime dead

Hours spent
      —leaning on his cane
       grandfather waited—
   warm sun of autumn chill—
procession stretching up the hill
   in slow camera motion—
     wave—
     to him a hero—
      wave—
   head bobbing in recognition
of unknown sons—
    medals earned—
     where?
       Bastogne
       snow-filled woods
       boots worn thin
       cold, bleeding feet
         bronze valor
           row on white

  Row
     on.
Long tubes—
   assembled in Watertown—
to hurl projectiles
filled with furies
   across rebuilding germanies
to kill
   poles,
     czechs,

                    ukranians—
Insured democracies
on scorched technology.
Uncle,
         he had been too old,
marveled
         until his hippie son
         Cried
being very young
                    and
                              terrified.
He never
         sought
                   gainful
                   Employ
meant something more
         than beaches
                   open for the summer
while we
         marched—
                   red capes and felt hats—
along the broad way
         passed grandfather's empty house
         in nodded recognition
but how would I have voted?
                   I met him
years later
brunch
incoherent speaker
         the day when
                   John-John cried.
Coincidence? —

we waved
        in slow camera motion—
as you
        came
            long procession stretching up the hill
                and grandfather
                    leaned on his cane
            to wave
                and told me
                    stand small boy straight
for heroes who had fought
        those living
            and those dead
and grandfather
        for whom I
            dread filled
        cried
            as in band wool we marched
            by.
                    good-bye.

Lies

At the Arab café, the old woman
serves me sweet, spiced coffee
boiled in a brass *dallah*
and dainty baklava:
flaky pastry, sticky with honey,
rich with pistachios,
and just a hint of rosewater.

Holding time in the moment,
I look at her worn hands,
beneath her hajib, the creases in her face.

      Ma, my mother's mother, had wrinkles.
      Just such a smile as she served me *kugel*,
      borscht, gefilte fish: made with her own
      worn hands.

They speak Arabic,
as my parents and grandparents used Yiddish
to hide concerns and jokes from me.
      Sometimes, Ma would translate,
      always with a wry smile
      that said don't tell your mother.
          She left out the things I should not hear.

Ma and Pa were the emotional mainstay of my life.
When they left for Arizona,
               we went to the airport.

I brought my favorite toy, a stuffed, black dog.

He, too, wanted to say goodbye.

My mother gave the dog to my cousin.
          "You're too big," she said.
That night, I crawled under covers and cried
                              for both losses.

          They didn't like the southwest. Too dry. Too hot.
          Too far from people they loved.

          My uncle, the éclair-eating doctor,
          gave them an apartment.

          Pa and I stood on Broadway to watch
          Eisenhower's victorious cavalcade.

          When Pa died, my mother went off to meet
                    family.
          Knowing they'd return, I set the dining room,
          made coffee, put out what sweets we had.

          Furious, Mom said,
                    "Don't you realize my father has died?"
          She cleared away what I had done.
                    "I was trying to—"
                         "Go to bed."
          She laid the table, refilled the percolator, offered
                    refreshments.
                              Mourning must have its suffering,
                                   pain its grief.

Baruch eloheinu Baruch adoneinu

Baruch malkeinu Baruch moshieinu

Saturday mornings at camp we made believe
we believed in a god who would send a savior.

     Ma's funeral was the first I was allowed to
          attend.

     While their wives mourned, my father and Uncle
     Robert came to collect me
          from the reluctancy of boarding school.

     "Have him back for vespers," the headmaster
          instructed;
     not a word of condolence or any words to me.

     On the ride to Boston, they talked
     about a new sound system for the camp;
          better to ignore me in the back seat.

     Watching winter's bereavement
     through the steamed window
          I thought of junior high.
     After school, I'd walk to Ma's apartment.
          We'd play canasta. She'd talk about the
     cleaning that needed doing.
     I'd let her win
             and never offered to help.
How could I diminish the power of guilt?

     Some nights at home, I'd find my mother
          washing floors on her knees.

Her form of prayer;
        she never went to *shul*.

At the gravesite, the sialoquent rabbi
    spoke of the Titanic, icebergs,
        and the unpredictability of death.
          We'd been predicting my
    grandmother's passing for years.
    He rode back from the service with us and
joked about eating lobsters
        and the foolishness of faith.
Each sibilant filled the passenger compartment
    with saliva spray.
I tried to find meaning:
    that there was no savior;
    that we need to build our own lifeboats?

Yisgadal v'yiskadash shmay raboh
    Exalted and hallowed be His name,
        which we are never allowed to say.

At vespers, one of the faculty talks about
        the truth to be found within. Phineas
        Parkhurst Quimby, was Don related to the
        famous transcendentalist? Can the mind
        really cure the body?
          Is death the same as giving up?

When Dad gave a sermon on a Saturday morning, he
always told the same apocryphal story.
A common soldier saves the day.

Persevering against all odds, he delivers the
crucial message.
                    Horatio Alger would have been proud.

None of the teachers or students asked where I
had been.
                    I wouldn't have answered if they had.
                    I cannot sleep that night.
                              I stare at the ceiling
                    and imagine the floor of
                    the farmhouse in Maine.
                              I wish I could scrub
                    it clean,
                              of what, of whom?

First period French.
         "Bonjour à toute la classe. As-tu passé un bon
              Dimanche?"
         "Oui, professeur. C'était une très bonne journeé."
         Years later, sitting at a café on Avenue St.
Germain, I realize the teacher's accent was not proper
Parisian.
                    It no longer matters.
                    Few things do.
         That morning it was all I had to hang on to:
              the lie that it had been a good day.
                    When did lies become lifeboats?

I press an extra bill into the café owner's hand
and gesture to the old woman.
         "My mother,"
              he answers to my unasked question.

               "How do you say grandmother in
Arabic?"
              "*Jida.*"
                    "*Jida,* " I repeat.
                         He nods assent.
                            Jida, the
word tastes faintly of rosewater
                    and of tears.

The Women of the Hartford Community Church

They wore unflattering Simplicity
patterns sewn at home on treadled Singers -
faded cottons bought at Cole's or Maynard's,
general stores where bolts stood in corners
next to picks behind the post hole diggers.

It wasn't a fashion statement they all looked alike;
one pattern made the rounds at Sunday church
until somebody had to go to Lewiston or Livermore
with enough extra to indulge herself at Sears.

It was before the time of Mary Kay;
their faces luminous
with hard work grooves etched by garden sun.

Weed pulled hands cracked and worn dry
constantly adjusted bonnets tied
under firm and thin set chins.

They died in childbirth attended by each other
and were remembered on Wednesday nights
when the ladies' auxiliary met to pray
and drink their tea from Wilma's china cups

held with pinkies out while they discussed
recipes for pickled squash
and how best preserve the berries
their daughters brought
from secret places along the walls of rock.

At night, when no one heard, they'd pray
to thank their savior for *this day* never to request
a different life, an easier task. But sometimes
in a whisper ask, *if it is your holy will,*
might I have a store-bought dress.

Engraved

Snugged near the spot where two paths diverged,
between halves of a giant rock split by nature—
water seeped and frozen over centuries—
a blackberry bush and I wedged from view,
a boy who did not wish to be sought.

Above, cloud animals raced an azure course:
a great bird, gray and ominous.
Did she covet the purple juice running down my chin?
Did that dragon breathing pine-scented smoke
spy my secret granite place?

Pockets held childhood treasures:
garnets, mica, a dead beetle, a ball of string,
an eight-penny nail good for the task—
between tart berries—scrape initials
inside that close clandestine cleft.

Years later, I return. Our name remained;
not our ownership. Sold over and again.
But the faux Indian name, Camp Wekeela—
family, brother, self—witnessed
by a wooden sign along the new paved road.

I wander down the hill,
stop where those paths diverged.
Where is that cloven rock?
I have not forgotten the spot.
A small pavilion, not a folly just utility,
storage, slapped wood set on rough cement.

Overhead, the sky is pure Jhelum blue,
not a cloud in view. My thoughts race
across the scrim of memory,
origami into their hidden boyhood frame,
taste tart blackberries once again.

Festival of lights

I spun my dreidel:
Nes Gadol Hayah Sham—
a great miracle happened there.

What no gelt this night?
I lit the shamash,
blessed the candles,

waited for Presence.
God has forgotten us;
no gelt tonight.

Baruch atah, Adonai
Eloheinu, Melech haolam,
asher kid'shanu b'mitzvotsuv

God, you honor us with instructions.
Each candle a miracle;
Grandma's latkes didn't burn.

The old man at the back gate
brought oil for the Maccabees.
Miracles for politicians:

hold the sun in place,
raise the dead,
cure lepers with a piece of fish...

Real miracles are little things:
a piece of meat in your soup—
Auschwitz, Dachau, Bergen-Belsen.

The boy looks in a shop window;

a soldier marches, beats
his drum. Goosestep

Ashes blow on a dark wind.
Shema, Yisrael, the Lord is one;
what He writes is eternal

memories of survivors.
Rachel weeps for her children;
beware you have been spared.

Adonai is a moody father.
King of our universe.
The temple torn down!

The menorah lost to Rome;
perhaps the pope has kept it
or was it melted for gelt?

That year we celebrated Christmas;
the neighbors approved.
Once I sang carols on Beacon Hill.

Guilt this night.

à quoi bon

I wake during the night and argue with ghosts
demand admissions
ask explanations
beg for reconciliation

à quoi bon
is there ever a point
who is good enough
to earn never unconditional love

at three my father gave me
a Stanford-Binet   a test to predict
adequacy in school
muttered to Mom about weaknesses
lied and told me it was just a game

never allowed me to help
never showed me how to use the toys
he bought to remediate my limited
perceptual-motor skills

à quoi bon

at least my brother enjoyed
making things with him
while my mother insisted
I was sick or too young

she needed me ill   ill enough
to get attention   ill

enough to feel desperate need
to please
ill enough to give her peace

so much easier for her
if I would do her will   never
question embarrass have a say
so I lay getting well from
never being sick
while others took my place

à quoi bon

in the end both are ghosts
and I argue with the dead
can the dead hear
do they have ears
did they
          when living
                    care

I do not visit the cemetery
they were not buried with a spoon
to dig their passage to Jerusalem

when the messiah comes
let them remain unsaved

aleym ayenm devresheym yeshev'eh
gods do not require salvation

Beacon

Riding home from my cousin's fourth birthday,
the oil refinery's flare pipe's yellow flame
offered an otherworldly beacon
across Lynn Marsh.

Our pickup truck spun by a drunk driver.
Dad, changing the flat rear tire, escaped,
the spare having rolled away.

Mom hospitalized, I spent a week
at bustling Aunt Bea and quiet Uncle Robert's,
tucked to sleep on their grey sofa,
dreaming of my distant home planet,
the one from which I must have been exiled.

Would the mothership return?
Would my real parents come?

        I missed Theresa, the blonde—
        haired girl who lived up School Street
        and loved comic books as much as I.

        Together we shouted *Shazam*
        and waited for transubstantiation
        or a spaceship to appear.

        Mom didn't approve
        of my interest in a shiksa,
        not even as a kid. She hand-

picked Judy and Debora
who lived next door.

We played school,
doctor, and married family;
climbed onto the garage
roof and kissed;
I gagged on their tongues
and the thought of babies.

What do children know of marriage?
Mom insisted Theresa was dirty.
Kosher and treyf, Jewish and goyim:
what does a mother know of Biblical
            distinctions?

Bea assured me my mother would survive.
Robert said don't worry.
They didn't understand my real concern.
I could do without Mom, but
        I missed Theresa.
        I longed for that other world
        from which she and I had come.

For years, we'd drive past
the refinery with its yellow flare.

In my head I'd cry *Shazam.*

        I wonder where Theresa went.
        Did she find the road home?
                a beacon to the so very far away…

**Reflection on the Battle of Bunker Hill and all those
that came after**

In sixth grade we took a class trip
to a sacred place.
Anthony and I held hands and swore
we would remain friends
even though the next year
we would go to different schools.

This is where the colonists took their stand.
The woman wielded a pointer as if it were a sword.
Down there the British soldiers massed.

What did General Putnam command? Our teacher asked.
Don't fire till you see the whites of their eyes, we all
replied.

Poor bastards, my best friend whispered in my ear.

      Poor bastards
      battled at Breed's Hill,
      just a minor miscalculation
      like much of history
      hit or miss. It's not so much
      what we've told ourselves
      as who has paid the price.
      The grunts don't get to see
      big pictures, just whites
      in some other nobody's eyes,
      the red that soaks the ground,
      and the trench in which

so many die.
The rocks and dirt
don't care what lines we humans draw,
what battles we declare we've won or lost.
The red that dyes today,
the sight that's gone.
The dead don't give a damn
who's won because they,
poor bastards, all have lost;
those poor bastards, all of them are gone.

Anthony bought me socks for my tenth birthday,
came to my house, we played monopoly.
When he left my mother—deep in arbitrary rules
and sanitary fears—said he was never to return.
Using rubber gloves, she took that pair of socks,
still in Woolworth wrappings, and threw them
in the garbage. *Throw them out now,* she commanded.

I wish I had snuck them out of that paper bag
and worn them the next day. I wanted Anthony
to know they mattered. A small gift, but
in our town such things counted.

How many British did we kill? the guide asked.
Her voice savored the carnage. *Killing is wrong,*
Anthony whispered in my ear. *That's why
I want to be a priest.*

The last I heard … my friend, poor bastard,
had died in Vietnam.

Security Question

"What was your first concert?"
       An easy security question for those younger.
           Metallica, Zeppelin, Zappa, Hendrix,
       Nugent, Alabama.

Attilio Poto, my clarinet teacher,
       conducting the Boston Conservatory symphony.

           Mr. Poto loved long
              batons, preferably 3 foot.

           We searched Boston
              to find dowels
                         he could shape;

              just as he shaved my reeds;
                 just as he shaped me.

He insisted my brother and I attend—
       our first concert—the overture from Offenbach,
          Orpheus in the Underworld,
             complete with can-can.

My not-yet-teen toes tapped.
       I love rhythm, wanted to play percussion;
          kettle drums pulse paradise.

My brother studied clarinet;
       I inherited
          his first instrument

                        and teacher.

Attilio Poto, slim, stiff, elegant
        at the podium, waved
                beauty into being.

He taught me to anticipate
        fingerings, life, even love,
                but that night I could not comprehend.

At twelve who knows enough of love,
        imagine the descent into Hades,
                rescue Eurydice,
                        charm the gods with sighs—
                                clarinet and oboe?
        Experience the sorrow as she turns back?

Why do mortals ignore gods and love?

Turn childhood's recall to the salt of tears.
                        Thanatos comes too soon.

Years later in Los Angeles' Disney Hall,
        Gustavo Dudamel conducts Mahler's second.
                Pudgy, animated,
                        no baton—
                                connection
                                applause

    … comprehension

Heart still

beats
      Orpheus
           descends
                first concert
                    tympani
                        beauty
                          security
                resurrection.

Ice-cream Karma

I never met the man
who lived in the tar-paper shack
at the crossroads, where 2 - 19
ended at 1 - 40,
where we'd turn right to Canton
with its post office, hardware store,
bank, barrel factory, funeral home,
      and Thane's Rexall Drugs. Thane had a
      soda fountain with few customers and a stand-
      up Wurlitzer jukebox that played the latest
      songs six months after,
      one for a nickel, three-a-dime.
      Best ice-cream *sodah evah*.
      I selected B-10, my age, my favorite
      number.

I heard about him. Watched him
chop wood—his metronome axe,
chips flying, a rhythm of work.
Saw his scrawny horse
who never looked up,
not even if the brakes squealed
as we slowed at the no purpose,
no respect, stop sign.

He had a pig, too,
but the stye wasn't in view,
just the stink, and that fella
so mangey it might of been him.

In winter he brought the horse
and pig inside to share
the warmth. Nobody said nothin'
'bout the horse, but that pig
was another matter.
Shirley, the guy who helped
Harold frame the new cabin,
talked about that "porcine roommate."
He'd start to laugh. Harold said,
Keep your mind on your hammah.
Which didn't help.
     Shirley's thumb needed stitches.

          Don't eat like a pig. Dad was big on manners,
          especially when drinking ice-cream sodas.
          Sitting high, feet dangling, a stool that spun
          with the slightest push on the chrome counter
          trim, jukebox music strumming
                         "Sit still."
                    each spoonful, each sip,
               "make time stop."
          The Wurlitzer's lights—bows of green,
          red, yellow—pulsed counterpoint.
          Sip, sit, spoonful of rich chocolate,
          lick lips, look in the yellow-time-stained mirror,
          count something—anything.
                    "Please, time, stop."

They tore down the shack, what was left.
The horse escaped the fire,
not the man nor the pig.
     Somebody at Thane's told a bad joke

...'bout Chinese food.
Mom didn't finish her soda.
Dad did.
Don't waste.

At the corner a life's remains:
an axe,
an upturned log.
B-10.
Tympani of a job.
Mind the hammah.

Dehisce

A lowery day, damp and dark,
the wind, not knowing wither,
whirled driving drops of rain,
bits of twig and shards of bark.

The landscape—unnamed streams
and puddled lakes. Galoshes,
slickers, neck-dripping hats.
A day to stay indoors with dreams.

Huddled by fireplaces, games
and comics. No one read a book;
stories might hold attention
captive against the next day's claims.

I fled the farmhouse gloom to seek
a quiet place. Past the salt lick we
placed without blind or hide
to watch the white-tail near the creek.

A rustle in the woods …I heard
a doe? No, a dark pukwudgie wood nymph
in forest green gestured. I followed
through the birch and sodden alder.

Her pine grove of enchanted spells
gave umbrella canopy
and dry-duff couch. We spent
hours sharing secrets—hers I must not tell.

We kissed once but such a kiss,
not a child's peck. Longing
embodiment; imprint archetypal
memory burns with embarrassed youth's dehisce.

Whilst I dreamt, she went away.
I called, but she did not return.
Spirit met but once and gone;
her spell continues to this day.

Mandala

At the San Francisco Museum of Art
we watched exiled Tibetan monks
create a sand mandala. They breathed
in harmony with each grain's positioning.

I thought of the harmonograph
at the Boston Museum of Science,
where I sat on the edge of the wooden frame
within which the white sand traced
Lissajous figures in cadence with earth's
rotation. Mesmerized by fractal loops
set in motion by simple gravitational release.
I visited the hundred gallons of tropical fish
overlooking the Charles Basin and watched
Harvard crews keep coxswain cadences.
I wondered how fish avoided drowning.

I made believe I, too, swam
in a giant school of tetras. I did not
want to be a guppy, but a zebra fish
would have been just fine. To swim
with gouramies and angels. To feel ferns
sway with the rhythms of passing fins.

> For my ninth birthday, I was given
> an eight-person, aluminum, war canoe,
> a perfect gift for the summer sleep-away
> boys' camp my parents owned,
> but not for the boy, who would
> that summer be deemed too young

to learn how to paddle.

At ten, it was a b-b gun, which would
have been a grand gift were I ever allowed
to shoot. It was used by campers
too young for the twenty-twos
recommended by the NRA.
After the kids had gone home, Dad
handed the gun to my brother.
Even at thirty feet, the pellets raised
mosquito welts on my arms and legs.
Dad took the gun away;
admonished me to be more careful.

Cousin Herb kept his tropical fish in three
tanks and a Rube Goldberg system of tubes
for the nest builders and mouth breeders.
There were two half windows and no view
in that basement room. No matter, he loved
the science of it all. Enough to become an
engineer before he killed himself.
Perhaps had he taken those tanks
to Stanford grad school, he would
have seen a different view.
Who can account when paths diverge
which will be taken?
                    Herb did not believe in god.

At twelve my paternal grandfather died.
That was when my father spoke
about Benjamin, his younger brother, the one he
loved, the one who died.

We sat *shiva* at Uncle Joe's.
Joe, Herb's father, was a moody man. Herb
and I spent the afternoon in the basement
watching his fish swim. Two gouramies
kissed at each other in that maze of tubes.

The rabbi came and spit on us as he spoke
of ships hitting icebergs in the North Atlantic,
which had nothing to do with the dead man
who had crossed in steerage from Hungary
decades before. Perhaps it was the saliva
that connected things. Grandfather rolled
cigars for a living, such as it was
with eight kids and a wife who gave money
to every rabbi who knocked at the door.
      In college I smoked cigars.
      Each time I lit up, I thought of my
           grandfather
      sealing tobacco seams with saliva.
      I smoked Cubans, not American.
      Ivy League elitist snob.

For my Bar Mitzva Dad told me I'd receive a new
clarinet, the present my brother had requested
three years before. At least my teacher, Mr. Poto, would
be pleased. Mozart's concerto would sound
better in wood than plastic.
          I wanted to play
        percussion. Choices not allowed.

The teachers called them electives, the courses
I was required to take. Latin and mechanical drawing.

                    My father called them presents,
the items he told people to buy if they didn't want
to give cash or bonds to help pay for the party—
to which none of my school friends would be invited.
Only one fountain pen, a briefcase suitable
for an attorney, and a one volume encyclopedia
already out of date.

Rhona and Molly, two women who worked at camp
asked what I wanted, an unheard-of question.
A fish tank for tropicals. I could not
imagine anything more wonderful.
                    And, it was.
                              I took care
of those fish with determination. Cleaning the tank,
checking the temperature, feeding once a day, even
buying brine shrimp to celebrate each fry.
Guppies are prolific. Mollies and swords less.
The angels considered babies good meals.
The gouramies, unperturbed, swam
back and forth in contemplation
of poems I read.
                    They didn't care for Frost.
Poe was more their taste. *The tintinnabulation
of the bells, bells, bells* never warned me
of their coming nevermore.

The plan was simple…Herb would take the tank
for the summer. In exchange he would keep
those cannibal angels, any fry he wished,
and breed the gouramies.
                    We assumed the pair were not one sex.

Only, transportation remained.
Mom said she'd tell Dad, who was too busy
for conversations or requests.

      Fish die when the water runs out of oxygen.
      All but one died on the way to Maine.
      Dad insisted the tank had to come.
            One fish, a gourami, survived.
            Listing to one side,
his swim bladder gone,
he swam lonely
ten-gallon laps until
            I defied Dad, who said
it was my responsibility to keep that last
fish alive.
          Humanely, I flushed him away.
          The next summer the campers
had a terrarium.

      Sic semper sombianbunt et promis.

The monks at the Museum of Art
finished their mandala;
brushed the sand away

Everything is transient
      even the souls of fish.
          Did the last gourami drown?

    My rocking chair creaks
    I take the picture of my dog from the wall.
          Where is my cousin's soul?

Chuff

Some memories are to be savored in slow motion,
    preserved in the moment's scent
        perhaps freed by a single event
            to be commemorated in poetry's soliloquies.

Like the candelabra blooms of the hickory
on the corner of School and Evergreen,
the waft of lilac from the bushes by our front door,
and the clop of iron shod hooves
as the wagons passed: green grocer, dairy,
rags, and the tinker's cry, "Scissors,
knives, I'll grind!"

"I tended a dray horse," my father said.
"My first job. I was only ten. He dragged
me by the reins. I lasted a day."

When the wagons passed,
I could hear the horses chuff.
They'd nicker in complaint
of the hill, the weather, the load,
or just to pass the day.

        When I was eight, we had horseback
        riding three times a week at a farm up the hill
        from the Hartford two-room School
        with its bell to call children from their games.

        Mr. Wilson, his daughter Reva—who looked

like my girlfriend Theresa
but with breasts—
a pastiche of horses.
The mainstays:
Babe, the black thorough-bred
too slow for any race;
gray Snowball, ex-polo pony
rocking chair smooth gaits;
Paint, brown and white, from the plains,
preferring bareback, old burlap sack for seat;
and Chief, buckskin, tall, mischievous,
trot that chattered teeth.

Mr. Wilson had served in the cavalry
giving up horses for tanks and his marriage
to cancer. That motley ramada gave him
and Reva reason to go on.

Western, English, cavalry, bareback: we rode
around the ring. Walk, trot, canter.
Swinging my right leg over the cantle
an alchemy for inadequacy;
base metal turned to gold.

Sometimes there are cherries in the lemonade
        of life.
I was first to learn the rhythm of a post;
the snare drum beat of chopping trots.
The first to float with canter's flow;
the tympani of hooves on hard-packed ground.

"You don't need my help." Reva's compliment.

Looking down, I saw her un-haltered breasts
beneath her checked flannel shirt.
I blushed.
                    Neck-reined Chief away.

We kids rode to Wilson's farm
in the back of the black Ford pickup.
Bouncing, laughing,
        standing behind the cab,
        allowing the wind to whip our hair.

Some days there were drums of garbage
to be dropped, swill for the giant sow
at a farm not out of the way.

Mammoth grunts from mom
        and squeals from shoats.
We held noses for the stench
        even as we joked
                the sound of make-believe farts.

        The new green world is filled
        with sweet scent dehisce of flowers
        and budding leafs.
        The horse settles to his knees and lists.
        I scramble off before he rolls.
        The spring Vermont stream could freeze
        again tonight.
        I jump away from the splash of the horse's
                delight.
        My love laughs; embarrassment fades.

I take my son canoeing,
the St John's River flowing
the border of New Brunswick
and Maine.

We eat blueberry pancakes
and look for eagles.

His smile worth all the trout
we do not catch.

      Our first dog likes to drink
      Harvey's Bristol Cream.
      At the inn, they serve her and give me the bill.
      My Airedale collects rocks,
      hides a quarry in the seats of our Datsun wagon

which will be our son's first car.

We laugh as he mines her collection
from every crevice of the green car's being.

She does not care. We may cherish her in our memories,
but dogs live in the present.
           Off she runs
           chasing new scents on the wind.

      We humans cherish memories.
      gather them together
      as our last dog, the corgi,
      gathered her toys

> before she lay in a sunbeam;
> love splayed in our living room.

"I don't like horses," my father had said
when the question of offering riding
was raised. Mr. Wilson and Reva
did not last long in his world.

Reva and Chief lived on in mine.
Through adolescence,
her dream remained.

> In the nursing home, towards his end,
> redolent of detritus and death.
> Animals for the elderly to pet.
> Dad sat blind and deaf for hours
> with a baby goat nested on his lap.
>
> I do not remember ever being
> on my father's lap.
> I do remember his belt and fear.
> The rage that never followed rules.

The junkman was the last to ply our street.
Pennies for pounds of junk and rags,
while the off-black nag who trudged the dray
chuffed relief from each moment's stop.
Until, there was nothing but the absent scent
of horse, sweat, and manure
nevermore.

> Junk, the title,

one of my favorite, early books,
a collection of poems:
            Jabberwocky, Richard Cory,
            Father William growing old.
Irony too starched a name.

Through the shadows of night that cover me,
through the blink of street lights turning on,
I hear voices from my childhood,
        "I dare you to remember."
                "I double dare you to read a poem."
                        Memory, I am unbowed.

Home

For days I have stalled off not writing that poem,
the one about my mother, the one that tells my truth.
I do not opt to winge and whine or cover myself
with the dust of regret. That time has been spent.

I spent it being sick, first in body at her whim
and later in mind, desperate to cast off my child's
fears that being me would make her die. At last
I realized my powers were not that great.

I did, however, at the end, give her leave to pass,
go home was what she asked. Back to the pines
and birch of Maine—the elm had died—back
to the blueberries on the mountainside. Back

in time to a life caught in her web of lies or were they
cries? Someone to reach inside the madness with which
I had grown up. Delusions, recriminations, wanting
to know that the Black men she saw kissing monkeys

on the Weather Channel did not exist. The wisteria
she'd bring into my room to keep me ill in Boston spring
no longer mattered. The summer she insisted I have
German measles without a spot had not occurred.

I let her go. No need for her torment. No need to count
the madness of her life. I said farewell and called
my brother who claimed he was an only child,
so, he, too, could say goodbye. Two days later

she was buried in a stoneless plot far from those New
England walls, far from the smell of pine and the breeze
coming off the lake. She never took the time to sit
and watch the fish break water, the loons swim, the
clouds

settle on the mountain. I wish she had in the end
gone home. It is my dream. When I die
someone will carry my ashes back to Maine
and bury me there in the cool, crepuscule air.

Where monsters wait

How deep was once the ocean?
How perilous was once the sea?
Unknown dangers graved the monstrous depth.
From crow's nests mates
watched leviathans breech
and deadly doldrums lay in wait
to snare mariners, take them hostage
and bind them with skeins of fate.
Explorers lost even as keels ground
on an uncharted, unknown reef.

              My analyst could not comprehend;
              the pain of dreams and memories,
              my inward journey.
              Perhaps PTSD did not exist
              in his diagnostic manual.
              Sadly, his father had died when
              he was a boy. Still mourning,
              how could he understand?

All that now gone as satellites observe
the billions' progressing on road, and sea,
and high above. No mysteries left,
none unexplored. Only the heavens wait.
We will reach them yet, in ships
powered by a different wind.

              Now, my father is also dead.
              Sitting shiva, I said my lies
              and grieved in make-believes.

Nobody wanted to hear the truth.
Had I killed him at thirteen
would I have felt guilt or relief?
Better the old fire-axe be buried
in his head or that quivering poplar?
At the grave, I quaked with realizations
and grievances that could never be
addressed.

Where do we end up after this?
If not oblivion, please an alternate,
a universe different from his.
The silence would still be filled
with lies and platitudes.
Some questions are best left unanswered;
some journeys should never be made.

The dark space wind of questions
tug earth, sun and Milky Way,
launch mariners anew from harbors safe.
The universe spins out of synch
into the bleak, black, unknown abyss.
Who knows what monsters wait.

Kaddish and Amen

Ave atque defendat nos de nostrorum
memoriam de nostris somnia.

Hail and protect us from the memory
of our dreams.

Last night I visited with my father—
he has been dead for fourteen years—
recalled the traumas he inflicted
listened as he said *you have to understand*
When I turned away he shouted
I said I was sorry what more do you want?
The word had never crossed his lips
not in this memory   any more
than when he had been alive—
scolding, shouting, demeaning—
never once; only his mantra
you have to understand
No explanation was ever needed
only understand because   because he told us
so we'd nod and swallow
indignation, rage, pride hardest of all
This time, turning back, I answered,
you mean the sorry you never said?
I can play it back you know,
the entire conversation in my head
All those have to understands but no
not one sorry to be heard Still,
your question deserves an answer
what more I would want

When his younger son died of meningitis,
your brother, Uncle Henry, talked only to god
To his other son, the one who inherited
the business, not one word   Nor to
Aunt Peggy who suffered orthodoxy
where religion had never been before
Henry said Kaddish daily but found no peace,
not for himself or for the others,
those forced to mourn with him
Then he became a Shriner marching
in his robes and funny fez-like hat
bearing witness that the tests of god,
like bacteria, are ubiquitous
but that we cannot understand

Like your brother, my father,
say Kaddish in death's abode
Praise that god you never worshipped
like the poet howling, mourning his mother
more than once   for death
is not so final as to not occur in life
madness reminds us that cycles are ridden
as you taught me to ride my bicycle
in the park before the yelling began
Repentant that I fell that last
time and time again I did eventually
learn to ride   to keep riding
away from your rage—
more than I could understand

So say Kaddish to the holy blessed Amen!

Pray for peace to humankind Amen!
Now, I know why there is no god
why I must believe in him
why god lives on inside our heads
There is too much guilt to comprehend
Give us eternal pardon
Give us consolation
Amen, amen, amen
Give us peace from the contemplation of our sins
Amen, amen, amen
Each must pray for their own
forgiveness is not mine
not even had you said
you were sorry   when you did not
even if there had been
an answer to your question
to which there is only enough pain
for Kaddish and amen.

Surplus

Part 1: In the attic

When the war ended,
we'd drive to the navy yard
where Dad would peek in doors
and hand sealed envelopes to clerks.

A nation's war surplus sold
one storage unit at a time;
sight mostly unseen.
Highest bid took all.

Don Quimby, the tree-cutter from Maine,
came to Boston, smoking Chesterfields,
to haul Dad's spoils—cots, mattresses,
canteens, tents, mess-kits,

kitchen equipment: needed
for our family's sleep-away camp.
Some things, the unneeded, went into the attic
of the old hydrangea-bound farmhouse.

Not much use for cartridge belts,
nail sets, or mechanical clicker counters
used to tally those frightened boys
as they filed onto landing craft

headed to crimson Normandy beaches
or the spits and islands of the Pacific.
The killing done, surplus, unused

in a farmhouse, collecting dust

like rows of cemetery markers:
crosses, crescents, stars; stories untold.
Click the mechanical counter;
tally the surplus dead.

Part 2: But the generator was a find

There was no electricity then
along the steep-hilled, gravel road
past trees and farms to our pine-shaded drive
where Dad parked the black Chevy with worn tires.

Water flowing from an uphill spring,
refrigeration a canted icehouse
and propane tanks that made
the old gas stove pop when lit.

Enough to scare a yelp from Mom
that first night she lit the pilot
to cook our scrambled eggs.
After Horace Cobb, stooped,

in denim overalls and plaid shirt,
installed the generator, she could cook
after dark, but only for one hour
before the gas ran out. Enough

juice to light a perimeter under attack;
and a chattering sound to argue
with cicada, whippoorwills and the silence

of a billion stars I wanted to count.

Lying on pacific grass not yet hayed
I watched the pinhole camera of space
and counted. Start at the tip of a branch.
I never stayed awake past ten.

Part 3: Floating to safety

I called the skewed ursus-
shaped pond *loon* after the pair
who floated pacifically
across from our rough sand beach

closer to Berry's, whose herd
meandered to the shore to drink
in the afternoons before full-breasted
Rheba-Jane drove them to the barn.

It took warm, gentle hands
to pull those (f)lowing teats
while the great bull paced
from fence to stone pasture wall.

We flipped the webbed-ring life raft
and anchored it a hundred feet from shore
for swimmers to rest and dive.
At night the loons glided past

while the moon sailed overhead.
No marines had survived on our raft.
In the North Atlantic, torpedoed troop

ships had dropped such pontooned floats

over the sides for desperate scrambling men.
The Maine nights did not echo their screams,
only the soft call of the loons, who sang
a love song for Rheba-Jane and me.

    part 4: Ringing the bell

Probably meant for a PT boat,
the steel bell engraved *US Navy*
called the campers to reveille
and taps. Standing in straggling

lines, nowhere near tall to short, no-
where near young to old, motley
array joined by faux warrior head-
bands flocked on white tee-shirts

by a company calling itself Champion.
We'd salute *old glory* ascending,
descending the tall spruce pole.
Harrold Bryant, the laconic carpenter,

who believed less in God
than hard work and had fastened the bell
to the great granite flecked-with-quartz rock,
was there when the flag pole

had been raised. Harold reminded,
Joe, *fasten the pulley and run the rope
before*... Dad wasn't good at planning

ahead. Ringing the bell was a privilege,

recognition for jobs well done.
Raising and lowering the flag
an honor. Dawn to dusk, never touch
the ground. Folded to a neat triangle

stars on the outside. An honor guard
like those that buried the dead
like those who presented flags
to mothers and wives, to daughters

and sons singing taps, *Day is done
Gone the sun.* High in an elm
a porcupine searched for bark beetles.
Because he could, Dad shot him with a twenty-two.

No honor guard, no burial, no salute.
The body dropped into the woods.
I sat on the bell rock and sang
Safely rest, God is nigh.

part 5: Farmhouse in flames

Was it spontaneous combustion or
a camper smoking his marlboro?
The farmhouse roared flames,
topped pines and shriveled needles.

Maynard House, shopkeeper, post-
master, and head of the volunteers
wore a red fire-hat, black

galoshes, his usual plaid shirt.

We directed what water we had
to save the trees and garage. No
hope for the old house with its
root cellar and hand-painted

murals of Yankee soldiers, bayonets ready,
found under peeling wallpaper.
No hope for the last of the surplus
stored in the attic. The mechanical

counters, nail-sets, cartridge belts:
gone in flame like sailors caught
below decks. Field mice scampered
off to find new homes. Dad, a madman

with his Indian pump, rushed here
and there while the local brigade
watched and joked about who had brought
hotdogs and marshmallows.

The next evening, when the embers cooled,
I climbed on the bell rock and sang
Waltzing Matilda and dreamed
of the Southern Cross.

    part 6: In my sights

When Mom died and Dad, feeble,
needed care, my wife and I
cleaned out their Fort Lauderdale condo,

sorted—sell, throw, save—decades

of things. In the walk-in closet
we found papers, photographs,
date books, bankbooks, and records
waiting for a final audit

Yha shemv ketveb besper hheyyem.
I pray his name be written in the book of life.
Clothes, her mink, his wool suit, unused.
A toilet. Why? Replaced but not

lost in the jumble of his mind. Like
the attic of that farmhouse ash;
a porcupine thrown to waste;
a whippoorwill's keening song;

loons' call of memory's sweet embrace.
I spent a moment with the past alone.
There, too, I found a small wooden box
inside one last piece of surplus,

half protractor in form, used by gunnery
officers to sight the angle of their aim.
My world shook with the explosion
of memory. I sat on the unplumbed

throne and imagined battles. Dad
had wanted to take part, but children,
profession, and bad knees
precluded enlistment or draft.

Had he imagined, as I, battles at sea;
blasts of ordinance roiling blood
run water? Remember Doc Viles,
the stooped, stuttering physician, veteran

who cared for us in Maine. A steel
plate in his skull, souvenir of battle.
Doc Viles stopped along house-call roads
to gather granite rocks from farmers' walls,

to build things: barbecues, fountains, ponds—
peaceful monuments for those he loved.
He set them in stone just as I,
in words, create a poetic reliquary.

LISTEN TO THE BULLFROGS SING

Strolling through the park

I see her asleep on a bench.
She wears a blue, rag blanket cloak cinched with rope.
Her shoes are more tape than leather and mostly wish.
Her arms clonic like my dog's dreaming legs
as he chases dandelion spores in a perfect meadow.
Somebody's daughter?
Did they watch her innocent baby-sleep?
One hand hangs down; below, an empty bottle.
Who gave her that first drink? What happened next?
Questions. I create stories to explain tragedy.

> Days before, when we left that restaurant, a bum
> took my friend's proffered dollar
> said, *God bless*.

What would that mean to her? Should I wake her
and offer one of the Susan B. Anthonys
I carry for such a moment?
A blessing or a curse?
Perhaps I should leave it on the pile
of bits and treasures she manages
to carry on her flotsam journey.
Perhaps I should buy a bottle of better gin.
I don't begrudge oblivion.

> Why did he ask for a dollar for chips
> and salsa when we all knew
> he'd prefer a pack of smokes
> and a bottle of forgetfulness?

I do not forget her, but I do walk away.
I write a poem to expiate my guilt—
not because I kept that coin
but that part of me envies her.
Perhaps we could share a pint of gin
and frolic together in dandelion fields.

A Pendle Hill Grace

Someone chipped the way for me
with bits of bark and shards of tree
that I might walk this way with ease
and listen to the bullfrogs sing.

The sun is poling through green leaves
to bid me do as I well please
but pay respect to all of these
for God is in the smallest things.

The lily pond, the honeybee,
a child's laugh, an old man's wheeze,
the robin's breast, a soft cool breeze:
God freely gives them all to me.

Beacon Hill Christmas

And they, singing, slip and slide down Beacon Hill.
White-breathed, they carol as youngsters stop to gather
snow whilst grownups laugh and steal sips from flasks.
Ah, Good King Wenceslas.

From curtains, the ladies cluck and clack and share the
Christmastimes long past. Their husbands, wearing
waistcoats and drinking brandy punch, go to the wreath-
hung doors handing sweetmeats out to carolers, who
shout glad tidings of the year.

In the kitchen of number thirty-eight, Luisa bastes the
turkey once again and checks the yams. Marshmallow,
golden tan, the sweet smell of sugar touches air. A feast
each year prepared from recipes passed from Adams to
Lodge to Saltonstall. Uncle John, the patriarch, will
carve. Sweet Aunt Mary will ask a hundred times if she
can serve us more.

Memory is naught if not preserved.

Come eleven forty-five, we wrap ourselves and join the
throng that snakes to Old First Church, where, on
midnight's bell, Reverend Barrow once again proclaims
a king is born.

Kisses shared, friends embraced: back we go to gossip
about who has aged and who has added pounds. "Did
you see that woman's frock?" "They were holding
hands?" "I know." "I saw."

The children, only half awake, still they fight bed until
Uncle Tom, with a hearty laugh, reads again that
Longfellow poem and ends their night with "HO! HO!
HO!"

In the silence of a holy night, I remember what I create.
The Yule log crackles sparks. Shepherds, gather here.

Antique jar

I know not the substance you once held:
food or drink, poison or balm.
For the farmer or his wife,
whose work you did I cannot tell.
The potter's hands that gave you birth
have long ago returned to earth;
and you upon this antiques' shelf
have whiled years and gathered dust.

I make you mine to hold the past.
I'll give to you some humble task:
hold copper coins or paper clips
and feel you have purpose yet –
to fill your womb with any what
that I, your newest owner, wants.

Acero

On the morning of his last corrida
Manolete did not pray to the virgin.
What need for divine intervention?
From the vantage point of eternity,
Cervantes, leading the swaybacked Quixote,
laughs at such a hero's conceit.
Little boys with swords and capes, they
believe the legends of El Cid; they
drive the moors from Vietnam and climb
the mountaintop of Iraq, these kings,
who pissed the campfires of childhood
as if true manhood lies between the legs,
as if the truth of thigh and groin could
bleach the color from the crimson sand.

I found a strand of gray hair

trapped in a spider's web.
What tender breeze brought it there?

My thoughts darted here and there
wondering whose gray hair I'd found
trapped in that spider's web.

Old age had lifted it upon the wind
tumbling with draughts and gusts
until a tender breeze brought it there.

As I grow old such reveries
take hold of me most cleverly;
each becomes a strand of me
trapped in a spider's web.

A gust of sound from the palazzo

The laughter of children at play;
the music of water in fountains,
two lovers breathe as one.

On his balcony a poet jots in a leather book.

A boy holds a clod of earth.
Don't you dare, says the girl.
He heaves it in the other direction.
      Perhaps, someday they will be lovers;
      in his mind, they already are.

Valentino stabs cadmium at the indigo sky.
Too heavy, he remonstrates his palsied hand.
Tonight, abandoned to age, he prays for death.

The Monseigneur blessing wafers wonders,
Why do they never change?

It is such a quiet town.

Village song

The women gather by the well and sing gay songs.
They talk of the men who have gone away to wars -
far off and long ago, those who will never return,
which makes them fit for poems, loves and memories.

The not-so-young girl in bright skirt and peasant blouse
sings for her Marcus, a shepherd and her betrothed:
"For better or for worse, Marcus, you were my first;
I close my eyes and forget all other men;
for you are the only one who got the best,
in the goose-down bed I offered the best of me."

In the stables only donkeys remain fit for the carts
to haul virgins dressed in white to the fine church
where God will forgive their sins and understand
a cold night's bed and the hot desire of the heart.

The not-young girl in bright skirt and peasant blouse
sings for Marcus, a shepherd and her betrothed:
"For better or for worse, Marcus, you were first;
I close my eyes and forget all other men;
for you are the only one who got the best,
in the goose-down bed I gave the best of me."

The padre smiles from the lectern and reads
sermons that make guilty women sigh and weep.
In his humble cassock and beatific smile
he greets them and loves the sinners and the saints.

The not-young girl in bright skirt and peasant blouse

sings for Marcus, a shepherd and her betrothed:
"For better or for worse, Marcus, you were first;
I close my eyes and forget all other men;
for you are the only one who got the best,
in the goose-down bed I spent the best of me."

Dusk and lust travel together from house to house;
no one need know who has gone or come.
The children playing in the dirt packed square
never ask "Who is my brother?" "When will my mother
          wed?"

The not-young girl in bright skirt and peasant blouse
sings for Marcus, a shepherd and her betrothed:
"For better or for worse, Marcus, you were first;
I close my eyes and forget all other men;
for you are the only one who got the best,
in the goose-down bed I lost the best of me."

The women gather by the well and sing gay songs.
They talk of the men who have gone away to wars—
far off and long ago, those who will never return,
which makes them fit for poems, loves and memories.

The old lady having died, her rose bushes went to wild

Yellow, pink and red: once carefully mulched and
        trimmed;
now untamed, unfed or watered, and yet determined.
In turn, and one by one, they blossom.
Tiny, close-tied buds appear at the top of straggling,
        thorny branches.
Over days they unfurl, waiting for that particular
        moment
when life courses through each petal and calls attention.
For days, luscious and inviting, each flower pulses with
        the sun
and sweetly talks to bees and hummingbirds come to
        visit.
Rich smell of love and sex deepens its invitation until,
at last, full open, she awaits with no last hope of virtue;
ah, but such longing expectation.
Then, turning darkly, the petals laughing on the wind
strew the walkway with bursts of color.
The stalk remains, mourning death and wondering
if life will ever come again.

Lunch with poets

poets meet an invasion of words
metaphor weapons flying collateral damage

everywhere thoughts competing
images smells sounds serious damage

neurons challenged associations clanged
onomatopoeia archetypal universal schizophrenia

before gods spoke there was void on the waters
before words no sound of being only empty
vacuum abhorred bang of particles
hurled black holes holding time past future

presents wrapped in rainbow chimera ghosts
impossible poems written by infinite scribes

lost sounds of sex and suffering
words stream down mountains
waterfall splash of words drowning
bang and crash of death in sonnets

form over enemy forgotten power of verse
this way that and every word worn

thin badge of creation leftovers of gods' tables
asgard mead ambrosia fouled by death

heroes wage war with swords of poetry

Goodbye old friend

Hands too palsied to play,
rest now on untuned keys;
while music fills his head
with those lost melodies.

The salt around his lips;
the brine around his eyes;
the dark squint to the east
that sees no sun arise.

Lost upon an ocean
with only love to steer
this barque of memory,
this voyage of despair.

Farewell, darkened spirit,
go slow towards your reward.
The shell you leave behind
with shadows now on board.

I never drank rum with that honey-skinned beauty

I met in Saint Louie. Skimming her red hat
into the Mississippi floating on to the Big Easy

my dreams and you so sassy we never spoke
but you held my hopes. Mark Twain and watch
sandbars on the starboard. Corn mash poteen,
mint juleps, you and me, me and you, baby
drinking bourbon while steam engines hum
tomorrow songs in lives now passed. Dark
whiskey nights lost tomorrows, forgotten dawns.

Off the bridge. Crimson ribbon floating
railroad sparks and steam blowing
Screeching screaming. Hold hands. Remember,
Bridge arched Mississippi
Dreams. You, me, and dreams.
Gulfward flotilla dreams.
Fate cast sandbars. We
never drank rum, my beauty.

Selling the family home

the purple stain had become part of the pattern
something ignored by those who daily passed
only in my mind is it a memory of something so much
        more

we sat on pillows, our legs crossed, our hands fumbling
        for things to say
i wanted to hold and kiss you, but i was too afraid that
you would not respond, that you… oh, the love of you

the music had been carefully chosen, soft jazz, piano
you had mentioned his name and i had listened
wanting so much to please you and so, so much more

we talked of school, the teachers we liked, kids we
        ignored,
and laughed at jokes we'd heard and quoted
snatches of songs as if there were secrets in poems

i had swiped a bottle of cheap burgundy
from the closet where my parents hid their secrets,
boxes of yellow photographs, memories of youth

we poured two glasses, just half—the way adults
we had watched would do—swirled, inhaled
the cut-rate alcoholic fumes, laughed the way
        adolescents do

perhaps it was too much wine or too much more
the bottle upended, the wine spilled, the stain

my mother could not remove, so we left

a remainder of youth embarrassed, of young love,
of someone i would never forget,
and of something so much, much more.

Off to the market

My wife wants raspberry jello and asparagus.
I wonder if, despite our ages, she is pregnant.
Last time it was saltines and tomato juice—
always in the middle of the night
at the same time when later
our daughter would cry
waking me from fitful dreams
of the rock walls
behind my childhood home in Maine,
the ones my father
insisted we keep in repair
even though entropy
makes a better landscape
for poets and dreamers.
Among the coppice brambles
we picked berries for muffins
and pies for my mother to cool
on the kitchen sill
whilst she watched robins
nest in the apple tree
withered by age beyond fruit.
Still, who knows what miracles
can come from love…

'abla*

Outside the sultan's palace the camel drivers sup on
            dates and gossip
while the women of the harem live on rumors and deceit.
In her head the Princess 'abla pens words she dares not
            put on parchment:
"Please, mother, take me home. My husband does not
            want me.
He will let me go if father allows him to keep the jewels
            that came with me;
he wears them wrapped inside his turban—not close to
            his inconstant heart—
that he reserves for another, who has borne him neither
            son nor daughter,
but she is more than I for when they are together they
            make love and laugh.

What is the secret of her allure? Is it the jasmine perfume
            she wears?
The sunset painting of her cheeks? The black lashes of
            her hazel eyes?
Her lips scarlet rubies of desire, auburn hair, or hand-
            cupped breasts never sucked before?
Mine are greater and I have more, or so my father swore
            when he sent my portrait.
Still, no man has known me, no husband has come to
            hold me in the night,
no lover's arm embraced, no craving to penetrate my
            labyrinth of love.

The eunuchs laugh when they see me pass along the

palace corridors
imagining that I am one of them, a woman without a sex
          —without a man.

The roustabouts outside the sultan's palace, the
          merchants in their shops,
the artisans who make statues of the gods, even the
          soldiers who with cadenced steps
enforce the laws: all will hear the stories of my shame:
          how my husband does not come,
how my bed is empty never stained with my virginal
          blood, my womb untested.
They will bow as I walk by—to not would be to die—
          but they still laugh; I know they do
for what use am I, a woman who is not loved, who is not
          desired? Mother, rescue me.
Send your husband's troops to take me home. Send an
          elephant for me to ride
so everyone will know I am a princess still chaste but
          worthy of a sultan's love."

From the palace minaret the watchman calls the hours of
          the night,
invokes the gods to pour their grace upon his master and
          bring the sun's clear light.
'abla knows not sleep but cries; her shoulders shudder
          with unsounded tears.
What does Sultan 'aamir** know or care of her deep
          woes? He shouts desire
answered by aisha's*** laughter. The royal bed rocks,
          excited by such arousal
as brings attendants to their master's side with sweets

and dates that day arrived
from the oasis where once first man and woman made
          their love
bringing forth sultanic ancestors, their line direct from
          deities above.

'abla weeps, her heart now dried as raisins
made from those luscious grapes carried on silver trays.

*'abla means full-figured
**'aamir means prosperous, substantial
***aisha means alive

Old dog

Her golden muzzle gone to gray,
her joints no longer supple,
the old girl fixes a longing gaze
as she staggers down the highway.
Perhaps she knows where he has gone
to hunt along the byways,
that boy she's followed all these years
whom she would follow always.
No, she will not remain behind
although the scents elude her
and sound and sight have given way
to age and melancholia.
But heart and will must still give in;
to age the best of dogs must yield
and now he's with another hound
rambling through her fields.

I miss the general store

with its five cent ice cream cones
hand-dipped from metal tubs,
kerosene lanterns,
scythes and peaveys,
great balls of twine—
especially in haying time.
Bolts of cloth and patterns,
doughnuts fried that very day
in Mabel's kitchen down the road,
bought two for a penny
on the way to school,
and the grease would run
down my arm with every bite.
Notions jumbled with tools,
cans of evaporated milk and peaches
in sweet syrup, here and there.
And the old lady who knew
where each item belonged
because her husband—
now deceased—
had this way of loving
that made her shiver with delight
when, sitting in the doorway, she
would think of him and smile.

Burnished

My gay friend across the way
collects jackknives
by the score,
each in its wooden display case
hung on the wall,
each representing a dalliance
from his aging past.
Some are open and some closed
Being loved is easy he says
loving in return is hard;
did I mention I studied art?
There is only one sheath knife
cased in an inconspicuous location
my first he explains
first loves never dull
you don't put them away
they are in your soul,
your head and heart,
they remain burnished
until you die.

Country fare

Rutabagas smelling of dew-drenched earth.
The pistol crack of fresh green beans.
Velma's pies with strong willed flakey crusts
ready to dominate again.
And Clem's boy driving his boar,
one hand rubbing an ear to reassure.
He will not win and tries to not think
of the auction and beyond.
The doc's wife must judge preserves.
She hopes Min, his secretary,
has not entered her rhubarb jam.
Two neighbors argue,
as they have for years:
whose corn is sweeter to the taste,
straighter on the cob?
Their children grown and gone
live in cities where they do not plant,
except Gabriella who has pots of herbs
perched precarious on her patio.
They will return for Christmas,
cut straight spruce with warm odor of woods,
string popcorn garlands as once,
long ago, homespun people did.

Meditation on a new coffee pot

It has, I know, begun to rain—
    big drops that splat on window panes
        and run the glass course as they want
in merry race until they splash
    from the sill and to the ground.
While on the kitchen stove I hear
    the plop and drip of my new pot,
        a coffee pot with smells so rich
        to fill my nose and warm my heart
            with memories of golden time
            when hours crept and minutes stopped
            despite the ticking of the clock.
I pour the liquid eucharist
    remembering the touch of love—
        remembering the sweetest kiss.
Nut brown, she walked as if on air,
    her head held high
        with frizzed black hair
            defying discipline as she moved
                through the door—
                across the room.
With arched back and swaggered step
    she challenged me to not react;
        I failed her defiant test,
            reached out with moaning crave
                and sought her lips,
                    her bite,
                    her pink smooth tongue,
    in one brief eternity embraced.
It has, I know, begun to rain—

swollen plunging tears
    unrestrained
        trace the lines worn in my face
            and slowly join, drop by drop,
            with the coffee from my pot.

Hydrangeas

I cut blue hydrangeas
and one white for your innocence,
left them by your door, and fled.

You did not know they were from me,
which didn't matter as I imagined
you gathering them in your arms.

I envied the vase in which you placed them,
the table they graced, the window through
which the sun touched and warmed them.

They were close to you.

For August Wilson

I wanna sing
hell yeah, I wanna sing.
I wanna sing that song, that one song,
the one that starts in your guts,
that starts in my guts,
that starts deep down in those guts
and calls the world to know.

There are notes to sing so loud
they's thunder in my heart
and others so soft like a baby's breathin'
touches 'em and everyone.
I can hear them notes that sound like anger
and them that sound like love.

I wanna sing,
hell, yeah, I wanna sing
and I want the world to listen.
I want the whole damned world to hear
the tears, the pain, the joy, the laughs.
Damn, I wanna sing it all.
And I want you there
holdin' my hand and tappin' your toes
dancin' with me to my song,
to our song
to the songs of us all.

Dressing for Leonard (Bernstein)

Dressed in Goth black, with piercings, and chains,
Slick is ready for any Chiquita's games;
A bottle of tequila and a blunt behind his ear,
a tab of X in his pocket: he knows that he's prepared.
Cool, man, cool, he combs his black hair back,
checks the mirror one more time, knows he has the
       knack.
Cool, man, cool, the bling hanging on his neck.
Yeah, the man is ready, ready to hunt for sex.

And Jasmine in her flouncy, brightly colored skirt
is ready to dance with him, to smile, laugh, and flirt.
The scarlet halter-top she wears despite her father's
       words
designed to show off her breasts, she knows that men
       like tits.
She swings her hips, walks down the street, savors
       whistled calls.
"Hola, wait for me," one of her best friends bawls.
She smiles with painted lips and tosses her blonde-
       streaked mane;
wiggles those curvy hips to drive hombres insane

The scent of sex is in the air. The dance of lust is played.
Slick and Jasmine smile and kiss; these teens do not
       refrain.

Troubadour

Do not close the shutters of your window.
Lean a ladder close by for me to climb.
As the moon waxes, my beloved,
the troubadour and I come to serenade.

We hide among the willows;
you hear my lute call your name.
I will mount to you, my beloved.
We will cum in the moon's view.

As the rounded moon settles in her bed,
you and I will share our song.
My compadre will remind us of the hours,
his whistling flute will sing their sounds.

The troubadour will hide among the willows
to sing when your husband returns.
The cuckold need not know the lark's song
only enjoy the music he has heard.

I will leave as I have entered
through the open shutters of your room.
Having strummed and plucked your lute,
it will be time to leave with the moon.

5:12 AM

My love cries out in her dreams.
I wish I could reach inside to rescue her.
I settle for lying beside her
writing this love poem in my head.

I settle for lying beside her
writing this love poem in my head.
Come morning she will tell me her dream;
I will ask if I am the cause of her pain.

Come morning she will tell me her dream;
reassure me that I have not caused the pain.
I will want to believe her; will share
my poem and tell her of my love.

I will want to believe her; will share
all these new minted words of love.
In my heart I will hear the cries of her dreams,
and I will offer the balm of feeble words.

My love cries out in her dreams.
I wish I could reach inside to face her danger.
I settle for telling myself that all is well,
but all I can manage are these feeble words.

Age forgets
      but love remains in little things:
the touch of hands now paper-thin and veined
without such vanity as mirrors bring,
a forehead kissed, a sandwich shared, perhaps a tear,
remembered friends who faced what we most fear.

Beauty cannot fade when eyes no longer see.
and all that we have loved resides in memory.
A blackbird calls goodbye to me.
In love, we are forever free
to roam those joyous dreams that hold eternity.

Sip the hemlock's healing balm
and watch the pain of age fly free
on wings that hold sweet reveries;
we drink and share death's gentle calm.

At Giverny

        we imagined drinking coffee in the sun-lit-
yellow kitchen.

        We walked in shadows where the lilies swam in
deep-perfumed greens.

        I remembered bullfrogs bellowing love in cool
Maine nights.

        You exclaimed over the clarity of the artist's
light.

        On the bus back to Paris, we nested in each
other's arms

        while Japanese tourists asked questions and
wrote each word down.

Bookmarks

I used to collect bookmarks,
not on purpose, just tucked
one per book, forgotten unless,
by chance, I picked a volume up
to read again and found it there,
a little gem of memories,
holding thoughts I'd once let go.
Some were gifts I treasured
from lovers I had known;
and some were moments' trinkets
from trips on which I'd gone.
When I parted with my books
to move into a smaller space,
I gave them to libraries, but
the marks I burned to ash and smoke
as memories to let go.

Courting song

It's not my choice but yours
if we go to the dance;
do a samba or a waltz.
It's not my choice, but yours.

And when the music plays,
be it meant for saints or knaves,
my hand in yours I crave.
It's not my choice, but yours.

The carousel goes 'round;
the hurdy-gurdy sounds.
Will you mount my fiery steed?
It's not my choice, but yours.

The dawn may break the night
and we must run for home;
no matter where we roam,
it's not my choice, but yours.

It's not my choice but yours:
if tomorrow never comes,
if I should laugh or cry.
It's not my choice, but yours.

Is it time for tea...

perhaps a crumpet or a scone,
to sit and contemplate a rose
here in my garden all alone?

It is time for tea…
to watch the world pass by;
a bird chirps for crumbs of bread
and clouds drift in the sky.

It is time for tea…
to smell the garden as it blooms;
weeds and dandelions everywhere,
I must get to them soon.

A column of ants targeted a crumb of bread

Swept aside by a maid, they reformed and marched
          ahead.
Wheat or oat, rye or barley, they carried every bit;
ants in mass are so resolute that they will never quit.
Prizes encased in their determined, unyielding jaws,
perhaps they are the most steadfast because
even though the individual may fail,
as a group they are determined to prevail.
Is this a lesson, a fable, meant by gods for man,
that the group goes on better than the single person can?
Or, possibly we're better served if when
each of us should scurry on again
after the broom of fate has left our file in disarray,
terrified but trying still, each in their own way?

For Roz while listening to the music of Bill Evans

Will the music well when we meet again?
I can't believe it will sound the same;
I wonder now what will happen then.

Can you remember what happened when
The first time we met walking on the lane?
Will the music well when we meet again?

What is the secret message we must send
To bring us back that gentle loving rain?
I wonder now what will happen then.

If we can cause time in our joy to bend
And place us in some gold immortal frame,
Will the music well when we meet again?

If sweet laughter greets lovers in the end,
Angelic glory, a bonfire's flame,
I wonder now what will happen then.

Must that attraction we once felt now end?
Does such love have to give true lovers pain?
Will the music well when we meet again?
I wonder now what will happen then.

ACKNOWLEDGEMENTS

A Pendle Hill Grace, originally published in *Songs for My Father* by K. Weene
Antique jar, originally published in *The Aurorean*
Boxes in the attic, originally published in *eMerge*
For Roz while listening to the music of Bill Evans, originally published in *Songs for My Father* by K. Weene
He wrote to defy the guards and challenge the gods, originally published in *Voices, Visions, and Dreams: An Anthology* (compiled by Sharon Laborde)
Holocaust Rag, originally published in *Songs for My Father* by K. Weene
Meditation on a new coffee pot, originally published in *Poetic Realm*
Memorial for my grandfather, Ike, and the wartime dead, originally published in *Moonshade*
Silence, originally published in *Voices, Visions, and Dreams: An Anthology* (compiled by Sharon Laborde)
Waiting for the Messiah, originally published in *Moonshade*
Where monsters wait, originally published in *eMerge*